Customer Service Tips: How to Improve Customer Service, Part 1 of a Series

by

Rosanne D'Ausilio, PhD, Customer Service Expert

CHAMPION
FOR THE
HUMAN PRESS

ISBN# 978-0977236060

Introduction

The preamble to the US Constitution begins, "we, the people…" I believe we, the people, are who make the difference.

I am not trying to impress you, but impress upon you, the impact you and your people have not only on the customer, internal and external, current or potential, but the bottom line as well.

The interaction anyone has at any level with your employees, including you, gives any customer an opportunity to make a judgment about you, your company, all companies like yours.

70-90% of what happens with customers is driven by human nature, having nothing to do with technology. Qualities found in human interaction can eliminate much of the frustration leading to unnecessary escalations. Sometimes a customer wants interaction—not automation.

I often talk about taking customer service and 'kicking it up a notch.' In the food industry, the word 'lagniappe' is often used. Its definition is "a small present given to a customer with a purchase. For example, when you go to the bakery and buy a dozen donuts or bagels, you oftentimes get a 'free' one or a baker's dozen.

That's what customer service should be about--giving the customer more than they expected

Here is a working definition so we're all on the same page. Customer service is 'those activities provided by a company's employees that enhance the ability of a customer to realize the full potential value of a product or service before and after the sale is made, thereby leading to satisfaction and repurchase.'

Index

Tip #1

How to Use This Book

There are several ways to get the most out of this book:

1) Refer to the Index and choose the topics that interest you, or are plaguing you

2) Read the tips from 1 through 21 (from beginning to end of the book)

3) Open the book at random and read wherever your eyes take you – probably wherever your eyes land is something you need or want to pay attention to

And then:

4) Implement the suggestions, recommendations, and techniques.

5) Share what impacted you with friends, family, co-workers.

6) Positively impact your personal and
professional life.

My goal is that you not only enjoy the book,
but most importantly, add value to your life.

Tip #2

How do we take customer service and kick it up a notch? This is a big question so where do we begin?

 As an overview, it's a given that the answer is three-fold: People, Process, and Technology. Let me say right from the start, my bias is on the people side.

 My questions for you to ponder are:

 1) Do you collect and measure any data? After all, what gets measured gets managed, and what gets managed gets better.

 2) Do you have customer satisfaction statistics? And if yes, how and where are you getting them?

 3) Do you have ongoing training in place - not sales training - not product training - not protocol or rules and regulations training but true relationship building skills training?

Let's address the first question. Just because your system has metrics available to you doesn't mean you need to use all of them.

My advice is to start at the end. What are you trying to achieve and what measurement would absolutely reflect that achievement? Then that's what you want to measure. The first time you measure gives you a baseline, a benchmark, to use for charting your progress 1 month, 3 months, 6 months down the line. You're not comparing yourself to any one but yourself so it's fairly accurate. Yes, there are environmental or economic or seasonal issues, but you're getting a pretty truthful snapshot.

As an example, lots of companies measure length of call. Yes, this is a useful statistic. But if you are committed to customer service, then I would suggest first call resolution is more important than length of call. Southwest Airlines is committed to quality customer service and they don't even calculate length of call.

We'll cover question #2 in the next Tip and so on.

Tip #3

As we said in Tip #1, the answer is three-fold: People, Process, and Technology.

We addressed the first question regarding collecting and measuring data. Today's tip is about question #2 Do you have customer satisfaction statistics? And if yes, how and where are you getting them?

Most organizations have some method of measuring customer satisfaction. Customer satisfaction surveys through snail mail, online questionnaires, e-mails, follow up immediately after phone calls while the customer is still on the line, and random contact subsequent to any interaction: and, of course, metrics.

What's consistent in all the touch points is that they are 'asking the customer' as compared to relying on metrics only. Metrics won't tell you for sure whether a customer is or was satisfied with their transaction or interaction, but the person will. When you want to know about a customer's experience, it's very simple -- ask that customer. Metrics can give you a trend, an estimate, but the real truth lies with the person.

I'm not suggesting not to track and use the data, but don't rely on it solely as it may be based on tilt! Ask the customer.

We'll cover question #3 in the next Tip and so on.

Tip #4

We've answered the first two questions in the last two tips. This tip covers question #3, do you have ongoing training in place - not sales training, nor product, nor protocol, nor rules and regulations, but true relationship building skills training.

Experience tells us that 'people skills' training goes to the bottom of the list because of economics and the ever changing technology, product and/or service, software, hardware, phone systems, etc. However, that's when tools are most necessary.

If you were a plumber or a carpenter, your tool box would not be sacrificed for a new software program or a new phone system, would it? (I hope not) So why does this happen?

There are assumptions being made that people can talk, can speak, so why bother training them. But that's actually why. They are only talking or speaking, not necessarily communicating.

Communication means that a message was sent, it was received and it was understood. All three pieces made up communication. I recently presented at a conference with the topic "Communication Is Not a 4-Letter Word!" (meaning T-A-L-K).

In today's competitive marketplace, all products and/or services need to be great. That's a given. What distinguishes one company from another today is its relationship with the customer, and who has the awesome responsibility for that? Not your software or hardware, but rather, your people.

Many people have the attitude of "one and done." We had a program for our employees in 1998, that's it! Not! Ongoing training has many benefits.

As you can see, I feel strongly about this and so will address it even further in Tip #4.

Tip #5

This tip continues to speak on the topic of training. But we need to be more specific and take great care in the pre-preparation of the training.

We suggest the following process of assessment:

Analysis
Design
Develop
Implement
Evaluate

Today we'll address the Analysis part, and suggest you ascertain the answers to the following questions:

What are the strengths and weaknesses of your people?
What are the common threads among applications?
What are the mixed messages

(Chapter 2 of the 4th edition of my best seller, Wake Up Your Call Center: Humanize Your Interaction Hub is devoted to Mixed Messages – check it out at www.human-

technologies.com/book.html

What are the stress levels?
What are the current challenges - people, process, technology?
What are the changes that are going on in:

> Software/Hardware
> Systems/Procedures
> Management
> Logistics

What doesn't get communicated powerfully?
What is your employee's biggest gripe?
What is your customer's biggest gripe?
What's a typical interaction (phone, email, etc.)
What's the call from hell?

How do you do this? Observe, monitor, and interview your people. In other words, ask them!

When you have a good sense of the answers to the above questions you will ready for the next step on Designing the training.

Tip #6

This tip continues to speak on the topic of training. We are now on the D's (Design and Develop) stages of the assessment process (ADDIE, Analysis, Design, Develop, Implement).

Everything we learned in the Analysis state is used to customize and tailor the various modules appropriate for the participants. They could include any combination of the following::

Customer Service & Customer Expectations
Change Management
Stress Management
Communication
Active Listening
Rapport/Relationship Building
Team Building
Anger Diffusion
Conflict Resolution
Empathetic Responsiveness
Service With A Smile
Perception Shifting
E-mail Protocol
Language Skills
Common Phraseology, and many more

Each module must be tweaked such that it addresses the results ascertained in the needs analysis such that you are truly putting a round peg into a round hole. Otherwise, you could just buy off-the-shelf products. But if you do, we believe you miss the mark.

All role playing and interactive processes should be examples contributed by the participants of real customers, their issues, problems, concerns, and how best to address them as if they were the only customer you ever had. But more about this as we go along.

Tip #7

This tip continues to speak on the topic of training. We are now on the 'I' -the Implement stage of the assessment process (ADDIE, Analysis, Design, Develop, Implement, Evaluate).

To review, we have our needs analysis complete, we have designed and developed the training, so our next step is to implement it.

Because we must be sensitive to the need for personnel to be available for customers (whether they are internal or external) we advise training in four hour increments, with two sessions per training day with a maximum of 15 people per session.

Training is a continual process, not an event. Therefore, for impact and lasting significance, it should be delivered over time. We suggest 6 sessions, or 24 hours of ongoing training, per employee per year, delivered as follows:

One session per month for 4 months, one session 3 months later, one session 3 months later - or - one session every other month for a year

In this way, training is delivered in real time and whatever current challenges exist can be addressed and dealt with. Morale is high because people know there will be another training coming up shortly.

Employees feel acknowledged by management as an integral part of the company. After all, they have invested time and money in them, and rightly so.

Tip #8

This tip continues to speak on the topic of training. We are now on the 'E' of the assessment process - Evaluate. (ADDIE, Analysis, Design, Develop, Implement, Evaluate).

There are several ways we suggest for evaluating:

1) An evaluation form at the end of each session to be completed by the participant, asking questions, such as:

- What did you like the most about the training?
- What did you like least about the training?
- What will you do differently as a result of the training?
- What are at least 3 takeaways from this session?

The last two questions, of course, are the most important.

2) Benchmark your statistics prior to and subsequent to the training. Specifically, if you

measure length of call, first call resolution, turnover, absenteeism, have customer satisfaction surveys, etc., we suggest you pick a date a month before the training and then a month after and compare your results. In this way, you create your own benchmark study and can directly justify your training initiative to ROI.

3) Ask your customers. Let them know you have instituted a new training program and you would like their feedback. Most people would be happy to contribute their comments. This is the best way to get accurate information about the customer's experience.

Our next tips will drill down to the specifics of the modules necessary in any training.

Tip #9

Before we go into the specific core competencies, I want to respond to the many requests we received on the topic of Mixed Messages - which are rampant in any company today.

My favorite one we call "Quality, Quality! But Hurry Up." How many of you were told that the quality of the interaction with the customer is what is of primary importance? Only to be followed with, "but hurry up."

Or "keep your eye on the clock and move the customer through the call quickly, but remember quality is important here."

Mixed messages are commonplace in companies today, and are extremely stressful not to mention crazy making. It's impossible to serve two masters. It is not like there is something wrong with you.

Awareness is the first step. The more awareness you have, the more control. The more control, the more choices. The more choices, the more often you'll choose the right one.

As a bonus for being a loyal audience, you can download Chapter 2, Mixed Messages, from *Wake Up Your Call Center: Humanize Your Interaction Hub*, 4th edition at www.HumanTechTips.com/WakeUpChapter2.pdf

Because of the amount of space on our server, we recommend you download this immediately. It will only be here for a limited time.

Tip #10

This tip continues to speak on the topic of training. Now we're going address the various modules to be included in any robust training.

The first module is Acknowledgement. Your people are so vitally important to the success of your company that sometimes you forget to tell them so.

Their role is not easy. People aren't contacting them to say what a great job they're doing. Does it happen? Sometimes, but more often people are calling for one of four reasons:

> 1) Question - they want answered
> 2) Request - they want fulfilled
> 3) Complaint - they want resolved
> 4) Problem - they want solved

So we strongly suggest you acknowledge them for their incredible contribution to your team, your organization, and the bottom line. This can be done verbally, via email, by snail mail, individually or in a group setting.

Tip #11

I'm going off topic (but not really) to tell you about something that just happened to me.

I was away recently speaking at two conferences. Flying from Norfolk, VA to Baltimore, MD, I was seated besides two wonderful silver-haired senior ladies. Now usually I don't speak much on a plane, especially since I had just presented for 1 1/2 hours (without a microphone).

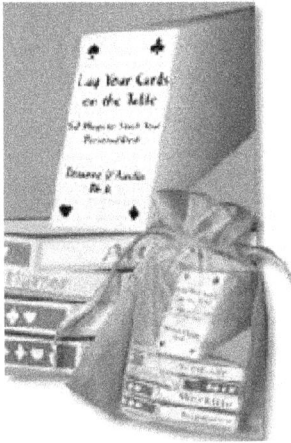

However, I was looking through my newest book that had just come out (Lay Your Cards On The Table: 52 Ways to Stack Your Personal Deck - now with a 32 card deck $22.97).

To learn more go here www.HumanTechTips.co m/LayYourCardsOnTheTa blewithcards.html

My granddaughter Lauren's picture is opposite the Smile poem (page 97). The woman next to me noticed the page so I showed her, well bragged about, my granddaughter. She took the book from me, read the poem, and asked if I wrote it. I told her I wrote the entire book and she shared this information with her seat-mate who I later found out was her sister, Anne.

They were opening at random and reading various humorous and/or inspirational readings. Why am I telling you this?

Because for the first time I was privy to immediate, spontaneous feedback. It could be interpreted as live monitoring. I actually felt like I was eavesdropping--and it was wonderful. Here's what I heard (by now they each had a copy of their own, bought, paid for, and autographed).

Oh, this is so funny. I'm going to love reading this book.
Listen to this (and she quoted to her sister)
Spontaneous laughter.
This is so moving. I'm enjoying this already.
I hope I can have this attitude some day.
The world would be a better place if everyone read this one.
What great Xmas presents this would make!
Can we buy more from you?

What are the lessons here?

1) Ask your customer! You want to know how you're doing? Ask your customer.
2) Give your customers value, and
3) They'll ask to buy more.

It's very simple, not complicated. 1) Give your customers what they want, 2) check in with them to see how you're doing, 3) put in corrections, when and if necessary, and then 4) be prepared to sell them more products and/or services.

Tip #12

This tip continues to speak on the topic of training and the various modules necessary in any robust training.

The first was Acknowledgement. Today's topic is World Class Customer Service. I believe in order to speak about something, we first need to define it.

What is world class customer service?

Those activities provided by a company's employees that enhance the ability of a customer to realize the full potential value of a product or service before and after the sale is made, thereby leading to satisfaction and repurchase.

And it is customer driven which means the focus is on what the customer needs and wants. Why? What will that do? Companies focus on the customers to:

- Ensure repurchase
- Increase customer loyalty
- Better meet customer expectations (next tip)
- Ensure a predictably positive experience for

The objective, of course, is to provide an experience over time such that the customer will view your company as their supplier of choice.

And the purpose of customer service is what? To retain customers, of course. A 5% increase in customer retention can result in 100% profits for your company.

Next tip we'll look at what customer's expectations are.

Tip #13

This tip continues to speak on the topic of training and the various modules necessary in any robust training.

The first was Acknowledgement. The next one was World Class Customer Service. Today's we're discussing Customer Expectations.

Have you ever heard a negative expectation on the part of the customer? As if no matter what you say, it won't help and they won't get what it is they are after? Yes?

Remember this. They are still initiating the contact. Therefore, perhaps a part of them hopes to be well taken care of, and you have the opportunity with each call to turn these people around.

So again let's define some terms so we're on the same page.

Customer Satisfaction: A state of mind that occurs when a customer's actual perception of a service or product's value meets or exceeds his or her expectations.

And, customer dissatisfaction occurs when:

Expectations Are Not Met
Promises Are Not Fulfilled
Perception Falls Short Of Expectations
Gap Is Negative

A working formula is: Perception –
Expectations = Satisfaction

Examples of expectations could be:

Reliability
Availability
Durability
Fast
Quality
Fresh
Safety
Friendly
Timeliness
Knowledgeable

However, people--customers--don't buy
products, they buy expectations. The best
products are designed not so much to meet
specifications and fulfill customer
requirements, as they are to **match or
surpass customer expectations.**

There are 2 key factor driving customer
expectations:

1) No unpleasant surprises.

Tell it like it is
Under-commit and over-perform and

2) When problems happen:

Take ownership
Keep your promises
Give clear, honest explanations
Be accessible, timely and courteous

Tip #14

This tip continues to speak on the topic of training and the various modules necessary in any robust training.

The first was Acknowledgement. The next one was World Class Customer Service. Then came Customer Expectations. Today, we begin our discussion about Change.

In today's world, change is inevitable, albeit very stressful. The truth is no one welcomes change except a wet baby!

On the one hand, change represents growth, opportunity and innovation. People who have this perception would be bored if there were not change. For them happy endings, or even not so happy endings, are happy beginnings or opportunities for new beginnings.

However, on the other hand, to some people change can represent threat, disorientation, and upheaval. These people see change as an event rather than a process. And they do not want to change!

People respond to change in different ways. For example with:

Anger
Withdrawal
Worry
Sadness

These are normal reactions. They are what is to be expected. There is nothing wrong with reacting this way. However, when someone stays in any of these places for any length of time, this could be a problem. But in the beginning, it's just a reaction, not a problem.

What stops it from becoming a problem is acknowledging the existence of whatever feeling is present. I contend that you can't go from A to C without going through B and B is the acknowledgment of whatever feeling or thought is in the way of embracing the change.

Yet people tend to focus on technical issues only. Why? Because they are predictable like planning, budgeting, or staffing.

Or the assumption is made that we all know that we can do the new job, learn the new system, hardware, software, policy, whatever. That is the intellect. We know how to take care of the intellect. We reason, we understand, and then we deal with it.

But there aren't a lot of tools available for the emotional upset and pressing issues surrounding change are human, or emotional.

The first step along the journey of change begins with knowing what stage you are in. In change, as in many aspects of life, timing is everything. You apply different processes to your problems at different stages of change.

Next tip we'll go into the six stages of change.

Tip #15

This tip continues to speak on the topic of training and the various modules necessary in any robust training.

Today we're continuing our discussion of change. The first step along the journey of change begins with knowing what stage you are in. In change as in many other aspects of life, timing is everything. You apply different processes to your problems at different stages of change.

Dr. James O. Prochaska, Professor at the University of Rhode Island, is one of the developers of the transtheoretical model of therapy and behavior change and the author of several books and over 100 articles. He has graciously given me permission to reproduce his material in my books and to present his work. He matches the process of change to the needs of individuals at each stage of change, and works in harmony with how people change naturally.

There are 6 well-defined stages of change through which self changers move:

    1. *Precontemplation*. The writer G. K. Chesterton might have been describing

precontemplators when he said, "it isn't that they can't see the solution. It's that they can't see the problem." Precontemplators have no intention of changing their behavior and deny having a problem. Precontemplation can be defined as not changing!

2. *Contemplation*. Here you acknowledge you have a problem or an issue and begin to think seriously about solving it, yet not right away (but within the next six months). You know your destination, even how to get there, but you are not quite ready to go yet.

3. *Preparation.* You plan to take action, so you now begin setting dates.

4. *Action.* This is where changes in behavior actually take place, and others can see them. This stage is very busy and as you can imagine, requires the greatest commitment of time and energy.

5. *Maintenance*. Change never ends with action. Maintenance is critically important to prevent lapses.

6. *Termination.* This is the ultimate goal for all changes. Old behaviors never return; you have complete confidence that you can cope.

Most successful self-changers follow the same road for every problem or issue. They do not try to skip stages. A key to successful change for any given problem is knowing what stage you are in. Although nearly all change begins with precontemplation, only the most successful reaches termination.

Change occurs on a continuum. Sometimes we leap, sometimes we crawl, and sometimes we seem to slip back. However, so long as we continue to visualize (contemplate) change in a way that looks positive to us and we believe it will happen, that change will occur. This focus is required at all six stages of change.

By now I expect you have found yourself, your co-workers, your peers, your bosses, and family members in this list. Awareness is the first step. In order to go from A to B to C, you first need to acknowledge where you are at A before you can ever move to B or C.

Tip #16

This tip continues to speak on the topic of training and the various modules necessary in any robust training.

This tip begins our discussion of Stress.

I don't think this happens at your organization but at some companies it seems the team you work with is reorganized, re-engineered, downsized, right sized or reformatted; that jobs are redefined; markets shift, and there are layoffs almost daily. New hardware, new software, even policies and procedures are in constant flux. Does that ever happen to you? If so, you're not alone!

By the same token, a typical company treats their reps, analysts, supervisors, managers, employees, like drones on the one hand, and then expects them to work service miracles on the other.

One consequence of this disparity between role responsibility and acknowledgment and support is job tension. No coincidence then, that research identified your job as one of the ten most stressful jobs in America

Let's be clear and define what we're walking about:

>1) Job tension is defined as work overload, ambiguity and conflict associated with job and work environment.

>2) Stress is the process through which you respond physically and mentally to stimuli, events, and conditions.

Stress is said to be the occupational disease of the millennium. There's not a job today that doesn't have its share of stress. As a matter of fact:

>45% of all managers suffer distress
>75% of all workers say their jobs cause them stress.

Anyone identify? More heart attacks occur when do you think? [9:00 am Monday mornings]   A recent NIOSH study said that 75% of modern workers (that's us) have more on-the-job stress than preview generations. This is due in part to blurring of the line of demarcation between work and home. Why? Because of cell phones, pagers, e-mail, PDA's, and answering machines penetrating or invading people's home lives such that they are more easily reached if away from the office. This means there is less relief from the job; that the unfinished tasks are always with us.

Stress is an everyday fact of life but, if not properly managed, can cause both physical and mental harm. When stress is out of control and we feel threatened and frightened, it becomes distress and can result in heart attack, insomnia, ulcers, hair loss, etc.

We go into further depth in subsequent 'tips' on this topic.

Tip #17

This tip continues our discussion of Stress.
Let's look at history.

Stress has always been a part of the human
condition--only the causes have changed.
Let's go back 30,000 years to when we were
hunters in the jungle (this is before you and I
were born!).   It was easy to see stress in the
body then.

When a ferocious, saber-toothed tiger came
into view, the body tensed. The hunter wanted
to be sure his spear was sharp. He wanted to
know where the other members of his tribe
were, and that their spears were sharp, and
that there wasn't another tiger behind him.

He received a physical signal to either run
away or stay and fight. That is how he
protected himself.

Today we have a complex civilization so it is
hard to identify the tigers, the threats. They
are still here today, but in different forms.
They are hiding in our offices, our homes, our
schools, and for me our highways. They may

take smaller bites, but they also take many more of them. The original fight or flight is no longer possible in modern civilization.

However, all the same protective responses occur when you feel your body is under attack. Unfortunately, there is no longer a clear-cut decision to either throw a spear or run away.

Stress management techniques originated with the concept that we have the ability to take charge of many everyday stress producing situations previously considered beyond our control.

We're going to go into even further depth on this topic in subsequent 'tips.'

Tip #18

We're continuing our discussion of Stress. For the record, there are two kinds of stress:

> 1) good stress, called *eustress*, pregnant with happy events, and
> 2) bad stress, or *distress,* when a person feels out of control.

Generally, when people talk about stress, they are talking about distress. For convenience and because it's common usage, I use the terms stress and distress interchangeably.

The first step is becoming aware of how you manage stress. The more awareness you have, the more control you have. Many people have little or no awareness of how their daily choices may be creating and/or contributing to a high degree of distress.

The five levels of stress awareness are:

> 1) **Undifferentiated.** All stressors feel the same. For example, a person who overuses alcohol to deal with stress may end up with a hangover which causes discomfort. This person's perception is

that it's the job, the customer, the supervisor, but not the hangover, that causes the pounding headache and sick stomach.

2) **Heightened awareness.** Here you have some awareness of stress producers. For example, you know the difference between a nervous stomach due to an upcoming presentation, and an upset stomach caused by the flu.

 3) **Personal understanding.** You know what triggers your stress response and you recognize your levels of tolerance. Here you understand the consequences of your choices. You know if you stay out late and party during the week, you'll feel lousy the next day at work.

4) **Proactive behavior**. You control some triggers to moderate or eliminate distress. You avoid consequences that add to your stress level. You party on Thursday nights so you feel good Monday through Thursday at work.

5) **Internal awareness.** You know how to manage your lifestyle. You know what to do to feel good and stay healthy, and you'll *choose to do those things on a*

consistent basis. You party on weekends only!

I want to help increase your level of stress management so you can reach internal awareness.

Tip #19

Wouldn't it be nice if somehow there were a 'magic pill' that would protect us from all of the dangers of everyday stress? Or perhaps a guardian angel who with the wave of a wand, would ensure that we would emerge stronger from every challenge that we faced? How about some kind of recipe or secret formula that would insulate us from the destructive force of 'things gone bad?'

Well, there is no 'magic pill' and to my knowledge, angels don't have wands, but there may well be a formula and it's no secret.

It's called the Distress Resistant Formula.
  You mix equal parts of:

> Optimal lifestyle
> Positive attitude
> Structured action

It may sound simple and in some respects it is. It's easy to follow this formula when everything is going your way. The hard part of building your resistance to distress, however, is to remember and apply this formula *when you are stressed out*.

Optimal Lifestyle. What do we mean? Eat tofu, drink only water, exercise four hours a day? No, of course not. However, individuals who are distress resistant have the following characteristics:

*Never smokers or ex-smokers. There is a direct relationship between smoking and health. Several years ago, the #1 reason people returned to smoking was weight gain. Do you know what it is today? If you responded 'stress,' you're absolutely right.

> *Consume little or no caffeine
> *Consume little or no alcohol
> *15 minutes active relaxation/day
> *20 minutes aerobic exercise 3 times a week (watching TV doesn't count)
> *low fat/high fiber diet

Now wait a minute. Before you say that doing all of that, or not doing all of that is impossible and takes all the fun out of life, remember two things:

> 1) Millions of people already live like this and actually enjoy it!
> 2) We are talking about an ideal formula. Any and all progress towards the

ideal will have you feeling more comfortable, relaxed and in control.

Tip #20

Today we continue our discussion of Stress.

Look at the optimal lifestyle list from Tip #19 (below for your convenience):

*Never smoker or ex-smoker
*Consume little or no caffeine
*Consume little or no alcohol
*20 minutes aerobic exercise 3 times a week
*low fat/high fiber diet

How close are you to the ideal? Here are your

choices:

That's me!
I'm getting close
It makes sense, but I've got some work to do
I'm a long way off, but I'll start now
You must be kidding, that could never be me!!!

If you said THAT'S ME, you already know the benefits of optimal lifestyle. Keep it up and continue to be a positive role model for your friends, family and coworkers.

If you are GETTING CLOSE, that's tremendous. Obviously you are being reinforced for the progress that you have made. Feels good, doesn't it?

If it MAKES SENSE to you but you've got some work to do, Good. Understanding the value of a healthy lifestyle is the first step. It sounds like you have already made some positive strides. I

If you are a long way off but you're going to START NOW, remember it is never too late to start; there is no time like the present. Are these clichés? Yes, but they're particularly true when it comes to health and lifestyle. You'll be amazed at how motivating your first steps will be.

Remember, however, to take them one at a time. Do things like reduce, rather than eliminate, behaviors such as drinking alcohol and eating high fat foods. How about putting that salt shaker away? No need for all of that extra sodium in your diet. Walk when the distance isn't that far. Park the farthest away at the mall. Return the shopping carts to the grocery store. I'm sure many of you do that now. Good for you. Use the stairs instead of the elevator, especially when going down.

This one is more for men: get up to change the TV. Yes, the remote is a wonderful invention, however... Try the smaller steps before you tackle the bigger ones. Early success paves the way for bigger and better things.

If you are in the last category, you must be kidding, THAT WOULD NEVER BE YOU, Oh, oh, pay close attention to the next tip on attitude.

Tip #21

We continue our discussion with the Distress Resistant Formula. The second ingredient is Positive Attitude.

We hear it all the time, "he's got a bad attitude." "If only you had a better attitude." "I don't like your attitude," or sometimes we simply hear, you know, she has an 'attitude.' This last one suggests the person has some kind of horribly contagious disease.

An attitude starts out as nothing more than an opinion or feeling, sometimes good, sometimes bad. If the attitude appears to benefit the person and is neutral or beneficial to society, it is called a 'positive attitude.' If on the other hand, the attitude is harmful to the person, interferes with his goals, or is potentially harmful to society, it is called a 'negative attitude.'

It's difficult not to let negative attitudes creep into our daily lives. Quite frankly, we shouldn't try to totally repress them. The concern, however, is in not letting these thoughts and feelings take control.

B e c a u s e negative attitudes affect behavior; negative behavior has consequences and leads to negative attitudes, which then affects behavior. Well, you get the idea. Negative attitudes affect behavior and behavior has consequences.

The ABC Stress Cycle

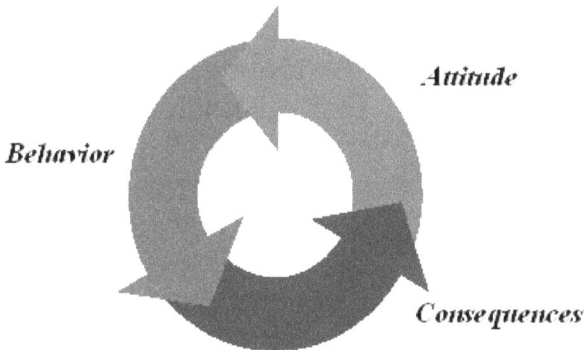

Attitude

Behavior

Consequences

Maybe it's not as simple as ABC.   But if you want to learn how to resist the negative impact of daily challenges, the ABC's of stress are just as important as the ABC's of the alphabet.

• •

Note: If you find these tips useful, be sure to subscribe to our popular newsletter How to Kick Customer Service Up A Notch at www.HumanTechTips.com

Watch for Part 2 with more useful tips for you.

About the Author

Rosanne D'Ausilio, Ph.D., an industrial psychologist, consultant, master trainer, best selling author, executive coach, customer service expert, and President of Human Technologies Global, Inc., specializes in human performance management. Over the last nearly 25 years, she has provided needs analyses, instructional design, and customized, live customer service skills trainings as well as executive/leadership coaching.

Known as 'the practical champion of the *human*,' she authors 9 best sellers "*Wake Up Your Call Center: Humanize Your Interaction Hub,*" 4th ed, "*Customer Service and the Human Experience,*" "Lay Your Cards on the Table: 52 Ways to Stack Your Personal Deck (includes 32-card deck of cards)—motivational and inspirational readings, *How to Kick Your Customer Service Up A Notch: 101 Insider Tips*, Volume I and II, The Expert's Guide to Customer Service, Volume I and II, at www.championforthehuman.com as well as her popular, complimentary 'tips' newsletter on *How To Kick Your Customer Service Up A Notch*! at http://www.HumanTechTips.com

Rosanne is also a **Certified Call Center Benchmarking Auditor** through Purdue University's Center for Customer Driven Quality. This certification training focuses on the access and use of key performance data to help better understand benchmarking results so as to advise on practical solutions for improvement.

She represents the *human* element on the Advisory Board of an Italian software company, authors numerous articles for industry newsletters, and is a much sought after dynamic, vibrant, internationally prominent keynote speaker.